Dividend Investing for Beginners

How to Build Your Investment Strategy, Find the Best Dividend Stocks to Buy, and Generate Passive Income

Greg Middleton

Table of Contents

Introduction

The stock market has been around for many years, giving business ventures and investors alike the opportunity to go on adventures that they foresaw as having financial benefits for both parties. For those who may not know, this model was created to empower enterprises to be born while giving investors value for money. So, it started with investors giving a specific business concept a certain amount of money in return for a share of that business when it is running. The company must see to it that the investors are paid; after all, they have a tremendous helping hand in the life of the business.

Be that as it may, an investor doesn't just invest in any business idea that comes their way. They are called investors because they are in the business of strategically spending money to make even more money. Therefore, there are certain principles and strategies that an investor needs to follow to facilitate a successful investment in stocks. These will be discussed in more detail in the book, so you can figure out where you stand before you pull out your wallet.

Furthermore, there are a variety of stock markets. These are all different, providing the investor with many investment methods to choose from. Some of these stock markets are beginner-friendly, while others are as big and intimidating as Wall Street in the '70s. Some serve convenience, while others are aimed at relatively seasoned investors. So, there are many different stock markets you can choose from, depending on how much you know about them.

You will have to acquaint yourself with various institutions, forms of software, and websites, all of which work as instruments when used correctly. The most important is a stockbroker—an individual or institution licensed to interact with stock market exchanges by buying and selling stocks through them. This guide will focus more on online brokers, offering a beginner-friendly experience.

To curb the costs, it will be crucial to apply methods such as the dollar-cost average. This way, you will only be taking a portion of your disposable income and investing it into dividends. You will also curb the risks associated with going all in (a highly inadvisable method). There is no use in risking your livelihood (together with those that financially depend on you) for a supposed big break. Investing is not the same as betting. The investor knows that it is not how much they put in that matters the most. Instead, it is how big the yield is. The result is calculated through formulas and seen in a company's performance. Various indicators at your disposal can help you navigate your way to the most significant form of return possible without costing you an arm. Achieving a good return on investment efficiently also proves sharpness of mind.

While a sharp mind will win you respect and a name within the field, it will, most importantly, be the foundation on which you build a financially secure life for yourself. As a beginner, it is evident that you would want to progress to a higher caliber. Therefore, this guide aims at serving you with the necessary information to empower you.

Chapter 1:

Kinds of Investors

Knowing the kind of investors that exist is crucial to putting yourself into context. Most beginners make the mistake of assuming that there exists a single highway to achieving success through investments. People lead different lives and, thus, have different ways of interacting with the same things. The three main investor types are short-term, medium-term, and long-term investors—all of which approach indicators and other investment-related information differently.

Long-Term Investors

Most people who are not well versed in investments classify investments as long-term commitments. This is because long-term investments are the most popular form of investment. Most of the advertisements and media coverage of investments are long-term ones. The main idea behind this investment is that you put in a certain amount of money, either as a lump sum or in installments, and you will receive double or even triple the amount after a certain number of years. Insurance companies have even gone as far as to name their investment opportunities after crucial moments in life.

You can invest in your child's tertiary education or your 50th birthday, to name a few.

With this form of investment, investors do not get to enjoy the fruits of their assets until they reach a particular goal. In most instances, a long-term investment goal is never less than five years away. There is an element of risk regarding long-term investments; the most obvious one is market fluctuations. While long-term investors are assured of reduced work in terms of not having to check up on their investments daily, they potentially face poor outcomes. A good example is when an investment goal is reached when the market isn't doing well, which makes the estimated gain smaller.

One of the most popular models for success entails retiring and then investing that package into long-term investments that also yield income regularly. While this is a tried-and-tested method of achieving success, it is a bit risky too. When investing in dividends, long-term investors will usually leave their returns to mount up in value. Other long-term investors even go as far as reinvesting their returns in dividends.

Long-term investors are divided into two groups, known as pre-investors and passive investors. The former refers to investors who seldom make a conscious investment out of their own free will. These are usually individuals who only have investments made on their behalf by the companies they are with. Even then, they are not entirely enlightened about their company-related investments. Some of you here might identify with these kinds of investors. Due to the nature of this guide, it is better to be a pre-investor. This is because you are an empty cup to be filled and equipped with all the knowledge essential to your investment journey.

Other long-term investors are known as "passive investors." These people usually do not have a problem spending large amounts of money. This is because these kinds of investments often require the investor to consistently invest capital in their investment. Think of a retirement investment plan. The future retiree has to see to it that they pay into their investment in installments. Individuals who opt for this investment opportunity are usually those who run busy lives with little to no time for gathering the necessary skills needed to navigate investment opportunities all on their own.

Short-Term Investor

Short-term investors prioritize safety, returns, and liquidity. Most short-term investors are active mainly because they must monitor the market to get the most out of it. Unlike long-term investments, time is not a deciding factor regarding the success an investor must achieve. Instead, a major deciding factor is the individual's skill, technique, and strategies. Simply put, your knowledge is a major deciding factor in your success.

Short-term investments are usually a means to an end for individuals with flexible time. This is not to say that they do not have much going on in their lives. Instead, it is to say that they can work around their obligations to make time to learn, carry out, and even monitor investment opportunities. After all, it takes a considerable amount of time and energy to analyze and evaluate a company's financials before deciding to go in.

Active investors look to secure their finances by lending a hand in effecting administrative, financial, and operational changes within the business they are investing in. These investors often increase their influence on a company through controlling stakes. If you manage your portfolio yourself, you are considered an active investor.

As a short-term investor, you are looking to hold investments for periods that are no more than five years. There is a sense of convenience in short-term investments that long-term investors lack. This convenience stems from the fact that you can liquidate your assets when the money is most needed. As secure as they are, long-term investments often penalize you as an investor for wanting out before reaching the investment goal. While this will teach you financial discipline, short-term investments are at your beck and call.

Long-term investors also tend to have conservative portfolios, sticking to what has worked for the past few years, while short-term investors tend to have more aggressive portfolios, investing in things that are giving in the here and now. Therefore, the risk you face as a short-term investor is high compared to that of a long-term investor. However, experts in short-term investments often use their knowledge to navigate financial security through recently held investments.

Most of this information comes from their own experience and the rules of their trade.

Mixed-Term Investor

Whether you identify with either of the investor types discussed above, this is where you want to be as an investor. This is the sweet spot. Investing in the stock market requires a person to spread their odds. It is like betting on the lottery, only more responsible, as it is based on analyzing information that signals the move. The sad reality of the stock market is that showing up with just one action might be your end. As a result, the mixed investor has a better chance of achieving their investment objectives than either of the aforementioned investor types individually.

Your portfolio as a mixed-term investor must reflect both long-term and short-term investments. It will widen your chances of success, but the two usually work better together than they do apart. For instance, you can target some of your short-term investments to finance your long-term investments. This way, you can keep some of the returns you make from your short-term investments as your own.

The goals for which most long-term investments exist are essential to life as we know it. For instance, everyone needs retirement investment plans like parents need education funds for their children. However, this does not mean you have to finance your living expenses and long-term investments from one pocket. Therefore, pouring out of your short-term investments is essential. You'll have more freedom with your money when you get paid, and you'll have a better chance of reaching your peak success earlier than usual.

A mixed-term investor has a moderate portfolio that covers both ends of the spectrum. Also referred to as casual investors, mixed-term investors have some risky short-term investments coupled with end-goal-driven, long-term investments. This way, you get to keep your ability to finance emergencies without having to disturb any of your long-term investments.

While being a mixed investor is ideal, there is no definite way of determining the proportions in your portfolios. This is because this guide aims to equip you with the knowledge you need to make that informed decision on your own. Because we differ as individuals, it might be the case that one is drawn more to short-term investments and the other more to long-term investments. To make a smooth transition from either end of the spectrum, it is crucial to slowly incorporate the strategies and techniques of your most favorable investment style into your portfolio.

If you are a long-term investor, it is crucial to take it slow when adding short-term investments to your portfolio. The same applies if you are on the opposite end of the spectrum. It is vital to remember that the goal is for you to see to it that you learn through experience the different ways in which you can secure your success. Therefore, to say that all investors should have a 50/50 mix of these investment types in their portfolios would also set them up for failure. Each portfolio should reflect this mix by the individual's level of understanding. This way, the investor is investing in a mixture that is most comfortable for them.

As you will learn later in the guide, being easy on yourself will take you a long way. Therefore, comparing your portfolio to any other person or expert will not reflect the actual weight and size of your progress as a mixed investor. Instead, your understanding level will be a true criterion for your success as a hybrid investor. Your understanding is the one factor that works as a force for your success. Thus, if you are well known for having beginner's luck, just know that it will probably work against you in the long run. Zoning in on yourself and what you know to be your potential is essential to seeing this guide through and making a success of your dividend investments. This is a crucial principle for all forms of investment out there. After all, the stock market is a place for the well-learned, which is why you have opted for this guide.

Now that you know the kind of investor you are or which part of the spectrum you occupy, it is time to narrow the knowledge down into one form of investment known as dividends. To jump directly into dividends would rob the reader, who is entirely new to the matter, of their chance to throw it all into context.

There are various dividends—all of which indicate the company's position. As you read on, you will find that some dividends are preferable to others and that your ability to avoid landing undesirable dividends will depend solely on your ability to discern the situation. After all, your success as an investor shows your relationship with the concepts and spirit of the stock market.

Chapter 2:

The Stock Market

The stock market is a venue where shares and equity of companies are listed. Simply put, it is a marketplace where companies list their shares, and investors come to the market to look for dividends (among many other equities) to hold. It is crucial, however, to note that only public corporations are listed in the marketplace. The marketplace is also referred to as an exchange or the stock market. The stock market is essential in that it creates a market economy that is free in nature, making access to trading easy. This means that capital can be exchanged with ease.

An exchange can be both physical and nonphysical. Wall Street is a perfect example of a physical stock exchange. This is the street where investments such as dividends themselves have been traded in massive amounts. The success that Wall Street reaped from stock trading has greatly influenced the field of equity investments in general. The nonphysical exchanges are modeled after Wall Street, only prioritizing a lot more convenience given our changing world. The pandemic, for instance, is proof of the drastic changes within our external environment that foresaw the need for more small venues to trade stocks.

The share, equity, or stock price is determined by supply and demand. The more demand for claims in a certain company, the more its price goes up. On the same token, the less demand there is for shares in a particular company, the lower the price. The job of a good investor is not only to put their money in stable shares (such as those with stable prices) but also to be able to identify and invest in emerging stocks. Therefore, the share price is often a reflection of what investors and traders predict.

It is essential to consider the different stock markets that currently exist. This is to show you know exactly where to go for an experience structured for an investor such as yourself.

Major Stock Markets

Auction Markets

Much like in real auctions, buyers and sellers are connected by way of pricing to complete a purchase or order. As such, within an auction market, there is no selling without first having a buyer who has placed a bid of the same value as the seller. The seller will establish the lowest price they are willing to accept, and the buyer will set the highest price they are willing to pay; if these match, the trade is made and dusted. Because it matches prices, this might mean missing out on behalf of the sellers sometimes. When a seller has set a certain amount, and there are two buyers—one is matching the price while the other is over the price (just to make the deal seem sweeter)—the matching price will take preference. However, the essence of this stock market is efficient, which is achieved with every trade completed through a match between sellers and buyers. It further saves beginners from direct interaction with buyers, which can be tricky. This way, you can trade the simplest way possible, listing your price and waiting for a trade to be completed following a match. A perfect example of an auction market is the New York Stock Exchange (NYSE).

Electronic Communication Network

This is a platform where traders invest and trade in stocks listed thereon. However, it is not so easy to sell on this platform. Firstly, an investor must register with the United States Security and Exchange Commission (SEC). Following the registration, you will be in the alternative trading systems category. To successfully utilize this platform, traders must be subscribed to it. Subscribers here mainly comprise institutional traders as well as broker dealers. Therefore, if you are an individual, you must have an account registered with a broker through which you will place the order. As can be seen, investments made in such a market are not direct. This also gives anyone new to the scenery the safety of working through registered institutions. Although it is a bit of a lengthy process, it is key to ensuring that you participate in a safe environment. A significant perk of such platforms is that they allow investors to trade even when the market is closed.

Therefore, you can count on not seeing a bar on your trade order because it is weekend time.

Electronic Trading

This is a more modern and relevant approach to trading, relying on the internet as a nexus between individuals, electronic communication networks, as well as other stock exchanges. This form of the stock market gained popularity in the 1990s, making it exponentially young compared to other physical stock markets such as Wall Street. Electronic trading cuts costs and energy expenditure for traders by eliminating the need for traditional trading methods such as phone and floor trading. This is all because trading can take place remotely, often requiring creating an account and a stable internet connection. All the saved costs and energy were then focused on facilitating instantaneous trading of stocks. As a result of all these perks, it is a cheap alternative compared to the markets that first explored the grounds.

Over the Counter

Often, over-the-counter (OTC) stocks belong to emerging companies. Therefore, the stores are smaller, cheaper, and lighter than those traded on other stock exchanges. This is the perfect market to go shopping for cheap shares sold outside of traditional stock exchanges. The primary factor that keeps the prices of these shares down is that the companies do not list them on significant stock exchanges. This way, they avoid the costs associated with listing their shares on the stock markets. These low prices would make for a good investment if the trader made a good prediction.

These stocks are traded by way of a system of dealers and brokers, all of which are positioned away from significant exchanges. However, because they are not on major traditional exchanges such as the New York Stock Exchange, the shares bought on this system are unlisted. This does not imply that they have fewer shares than they do now. This is like avoiding buying a house listed by an agency in preference to a housing scheme where you can get it cheaper due to zero-agency expenses. It does not make it any less of a house; it is still registered as a house.

Over-the-counter platforms are hosted on various electronic platforms, with one of the biggest platforms being the OTC Bulletin Board (OTCBB), which the Financial Industry Regulatory Authority manages. This body is known as an organization (approved by the government) that focuses on facilitating the protection of markets and investors. So, it makes it easier for legal entities and institutions to make trades on the platform, which keeps everyone safe.

Another example of this stock market is OTC Link, where investors can still expect to trade in smaller companies. However, these trades are at lower volumes when compared to OTCBB.

If you are interested in the cheap stocks listed on this kind of stock market, you will still need to navigate it through a broker. This is because small companies often need expert analysis and consideration before an investment is made in them. As a result, your broker will help you navigate the best stocks, regardless of how cheap they are. Nevertheless, do expect to pay more in broker-related fees. Expect to pay more than would typically be the case if you purchased listed shares. Furthermore, the trade order might take longer than orders on listed claims. However, the payoff is bigger if the small company grows more extensively over the years, and you increase your investment.

Types of Stockbrokers

There are typically two investment avenues for beginners. These are investing through a stockbroker offering full service or an online stockbroker. A full-service stockbroker is more traditional, often physical, with an office (or offices) located in a city. These brokers go all in, with services extending beyond dividend investments. They will offer you tax tips, retirement plans, and stock trading guidance. However, these will cost you both time and resources.

Because you are more focused on learning how to invest in dividends, online stockbrokers (also referred to as online trading platforms) are the best way to go. This is because, on these platforms, you can narrow your business of the day to what you want—dividends—without having to sit through other unrelated investment opportunities. As you will find out later in the guide, online stockbrokers value research and ensure that you have access to just as much (if not more) information as you receive from traditional stockbrokers.

Chapter 3:

The Nature of Dividends

A dividend is a term that refers to a type of share where money is paid to an investor as a return on a particular investment. The payment is carried out at intervals determined by the company that listed those dividends. The dividends may be sourced from different equities, which is why different forms of dividends exist. Various dividends exist, and the four most basic forms of dividends are discussed next.

Types of Dividends

Cash Dividends

These are the most common forms of dividends, involving returns on investment (ROIs) in monetary conditions. The investor has two options once the dividends are cashed out. These are to take the cash and enjoy the fruits of your investment. The second option entails reinvesting the money and increasing the share size (or shares). An increased share size means an increased yield once dividends are paid out. Depending on the company policy, the dividends are paid monthly, quarterly, or even annually. When investing in these dividends, an investor needs to read up on how frequently the shares are paid out. These are the perfect options for individuals looking to benefit from the fruits of their investments more frequently. A company can also decide to pay dividends on special occasions only. These occasions may include large amounts of recovery achieved through litigation, unusually maximized profits, or when there is excess money within the company's finances. Therefore, it is crucial for you to know when the company pays out its dividends before giving in to its attractive prospects.

Companies often have dividend policies, indicating what amount is to be cashed out as dividends to shareholders. These also entail the period through which the dividends will be paid. A dividend policy is a custom for the company at hand. For instance, the board of directors can recommend a special dividend for one company. This will be one that will be catered to the shape, size, and potential growth of the company and the financial situation thereof. Another company's policy might prioritize capital appreciation of the share price by using it to expand the company. This will prove lucrative to the investors, as the share size will reflect an expanding company. On the same token, companies with dividend policies view the dividend as a primary need for the investor. As such, the dividends are paid regularly.

By the signaling theory, companies that usually give out these kinds of dividends are considered stable. These companies have financial records so vital that they can carry running expenses and repay shareholders in cash.

The fact that these kinds of dividends are cashed out from the company's financials makes them a preference only for the established. There is no new business that would have to worry about money problems because its cash flow is too tight.

Stock Dividend

Cash dividends mostly come to mind when the word dividends are mentioned. However, there are a handful of other forms of dividends. Stock dividends are among the alternative forms of dividends. Instead of giving out cash for holding shares, stock dividends give out additional stocks to existing shareholders as a return on their investments. The company's dividend policy covers the amount of stock issued as a return on investment. For instance, if a company policy stipulates that the stock will be repaid by 5%, one stock share will be distributed for every 20 shares held. Therefore, if you have 100 shares in this company, you will receive five additional shares as a return on investment. While other companies set up the institution of their dividend policies like this from the get-go, others use it as an alternative to paying cash.

This means that a company that has not made enough profit in one year to pay cash to all its shareholders or if it has other use for the cash it has, can opt to pay the shareholders in stock. What this will mean for you as an investor is that you will avoid the tax that you would have otherwise paid for buying those five extra shares in the company. This is because the stock is given to you and not purchased by you, meaning you will only pay taxes once you sell the shares. This is an attractive dividend for someone who is looking to save while at it.

Although the dividends are not cash, they do have a monetary value. This means that you can liquidate them and enjoy the fruits of your investment just as much as cash dividends. You can even go as far as enjoying the stock dividends by liquidating them as they come, keeping your share size and returns unaffected. On the same token, you can also investigate keeping the stock dividends, which will surely increase your share size and the monetary incentives attached to it. However, it is essential to know that the market value of your old and new positions remains the same.

Stock dividends are essential for the potential amount of lucrativeness that an investor is exposed to should they hold on to them for the long haul. As the business progresses, you can count on an increase in the share price, which directly translates into an increased return on investment. Individuals who invest in these kinds of dividends save on costs associated with acquiring more stocks. They don't have to pay any transaction fees or fees for commissions.

It is essential to have investments in companies that offer these kinds of shares because they will automatically grow your portfolio for you. This way, you do not have to do everything manually, deciding whether to buy more shares and which shares you should go for.

Property Dividends

Much like stock dividends, dividends here are those concerned with giving out equities that can be liquidated to their investors. Property dividends distribute property to investors as their return on investment. When this dividend is awarded to its respective shareholders, it is recorded at market value. For instance, if a company buys a particular property for $25,000 and the said property is currently valued at $100,000, then the property will be recorded at $100,000. The company's financial statements will reflect property worth $100,000, converted into dividends covering that exact amount. The retained earnings will then be debited with $100,000, while the company's liabilities will be credited with $100,000. This will show the property as no longer being recognized as belonging to the company, handing it over to the investors holding dividends in the company for that property. You have the option to hold on to the dividend to yield more significant gains. After all, in the financial world, property either appreciates or is a means to appreciate.

Companies often go for this form of dividend if they do not want to dilute their existing share position through stock dividends. It is also the case when a company finds itself either unwilling or unable to pay cash to its shareholders. Despite it being argued that they have no monetary value, property dividends provide financial gains to investors. If you are looking to defer taxes, this is the best form of a dividend. This is mainly because you can keep the dividend for as long as you deem necessary without liquidating it (a process that includes taxes). Properties often found within this kind of dividend include the likes of inventory, real estate, and even subsidiary shares that the company has. These shares allow investors the freedom to take advantage of external factors to monetize them most efficiently. For instance, no institution or rule is pressuring you to immediately sell your dividend for money, which will most probably result in high taxes. However, it is essential to note that a company will only consider this form of dividend if it thinks that the market value is not only fair but considerably different from the book value. When a company does opt to pay your shares back in the form of property, it might be the right time to consider a halt to your investments in that said company. For instance, if you have been buying shares using the dollar-cost average and find that certain shares have been returned as property, it is the right time to stop the installments. If possible, you can hold on for a while to see the company's performance before commencing the installments. This way, you can evaluate whether or not you are putting your money into a sinking or expanding ship. After all, if the ship does sink, you are the last person to be saved. Companies often go for this form of dividend if they do not want to dilute their existing share position through stock dividends. It is also the case when a company finds itself either unwilling or unable to pay cash to its shareholders. Despite being argued that they have no monetary value, property dividends provide financial gains to investors. If you are looking to defer taxes, this is the best form of a dividend. This is mainly because you can keep the dividend for as long as you deem necessary without liquidating it (a process that includes taxes).

Properties often found within this kind of dividend include the likes of inventory, real estate, and even subsidiary shares that the company has. These shares allow investors the freedom to take advantage of external factors to monetize them most efficiently. For instance, no institution or rule is pressuring you to immediately sell your dividend for money, which will most probably result in high taxes. However, it is essential to note that a company will only consider this form of dividend if it thinks that the market value is not only fair but considerably different from the book value. When a company does opt to pay your shares back in the form of property, it might be the right time to consider a halt to your investments in that company. For instance, if you have been buying shares using the dollar-cost average and find that certain shares have been returned as property, it is the right time to stop the installments. If possible, you can hold on for a while to see the company's performance before commencing the installments. This way, you can evaluate whether or not you are putting your money into a sinking or expanding ship. After all, if the ship does sink, you are the last person to be saved.

Liquidating Dividends

These are dividends awarded for the last time before the company's existence is seized. These forms of dividends are awarded during the winding up of a company. A company is wound up if it operates at a loss or cannot afford to keep running and pay its creditors. It is, furthermore, wound up if it is found to be operating illegally. The assets that result from this process are then distributed among shareholders based on the size of their shares. Beware that a company can go into partial liquidation or bankruptcy, both of which are not ideal for you as an investor. This is because if a company continues to own or operate the remaining half (in the case of a half-liquidation), you will probably not get any cash from your investment.

In addition, should a company find itself in a situation where it must liquidate fully, you (the investor) are last in line. This is because the procedure gives financial preference to creditors first. After creditors, priority will be given to equity holders. Shareholders will be considered if there is anything left after the two stakeholders have been considered. In a situation where there is some money left after paying creditors and equity holders, it is often the case that the returns are just shadows of what would otherwise be awarded if the company had performed in the way it was predicted to.

To avoid finding yourself in a situation like that described above, holding back on investing in a company that starts giving out property dividends is crucial. Dividend investments are long-term ones, and an investment opportunity and journey are cut short because winding up is an investment gone wrong—no matter how big the last award is. Furthermore, investment is supposed to give its benefits to you periodically, so receiving a once-off payment from a company that is in the process of being nonexistent is not a good return.

Most importantly, investing in a company that finds itself in such a situation shows your prediction skills as an investor. After all, the main point is to locate wells from which you will draw your water for as long as you see fit and invest in those wells. No investor will go to a well that is actively drying up. Nor will any investor stick with a well that is actively drying up.

Challenges Associated With Investing in Dividends

Paperwork

Dividend investing involves a mountain of paperwork. The paperwork can culminate in all sorts of economic-related sources, ranging from report-season corporate actions to dividend announcements on their own. This paperwork often includes keeping up with jargon and crushing numbers. This can be an overwhelming phenomenon for any beginner.

Validation

As an investor, you must check in with the stock transfer agent or the share registry to see the amount that has been declared and paid. Secondly, you must check if the appropriate bank account will receive the payment. The amount of data included in this process is what makes it tedious.

Ex-dividend Price Drops

An ex-dividend day is usually the day before the settlement date for a dividend paid to an investor who sold their shares. Dividends that are in this time window will usually reflect such. If an investor buys in before this date, they will receive the dividend. However, if an investor decides to buy in after the stipulated date, the ex-owner pays the dividend. On this date, the stock price decreases by the dividends paid to the ex-owner. This also tells the new dividend owner that they aren't supposed to get any money back from their investments for now.

These challenges can make it difficult for you as a new investor. However, knowing your way around the resources at your disposal will prove beneficial in your journey as a dividend investor. As such, the next chapter will focus on the skills and techniques that are crucial in ensuring that any investor carries out an investment that is crucial to them. This chapter will be a reflection for you on what sorts of characteristics and approaches are essential to your success within the field. Be sure to grasp any mistakes to look out for as well.

Types of Shares

The main forms of shares available to investors include preference shares, ordinary shares, and differential voting rights shares.

Preference Shares

Investors who hold these shares receive preferential treatment compared to other share-type holders. Preference shareholders are first in line when a company is distributing its dividends. Even when a company is winding up its shares, offering them higher preference often leaves the other shareholder types with little to nothing. There are also cumulative preference shares, noncumulative preference shares, and convertible preference shares, which are all types of preference shares.

Cumulative preference shares give investors the right to receive any dividends in arrears before the company can pay equity shareholders. Holders of noncumulative shares, on the other hand, cannot claim any outstanding dividends. They are only first in line when the company has made a profit and is issuing dividends for the current financial year. Their holders can convert preference shares into equity shares (ordinary shares). However, such a conversion must be overseen and authorized by the company.

Ordinary Shares

Also referred to as equity shares, ordinary shares make up the majority of what a company issues. These are the shares traded on the stock markets, and the holders thereof have voting rights in company meetings. While these shares are entitled to dividends, the dividends vary from year to year based on the profit the company has managed to generate. When they receive their dividends, these shareholders are second in line, right after preference shareholders.

Differential Voting Rights Shares

These shares do not have voting rights as heavy as those in ordinary shares. Consequently, they are cheaper than common shares, with a value gap of between 30% and 40%.

Chapter 4:

Indicators and Techniques

This chapter comprises all the platforms and instruments you may use to navigate your investments. In one instance, you might find that a company you invested in is starting to shy away from returning dividends in cash. In another example, you might find that a company you invested in is faced with liquidation. By the end of this chapter, you should have a clearer picture of when it is green to buy and when it is okay to sell.

Metrics Used to Measure Dividends

For a beginner, it is essential to grasp the six basic metrics for measuring dividends. By weighing your preferred dividend against these metrics, you will see whether an investment is a go or not. These metrics may also be referred to as criteria.

Dividend Yield

A yield is the ratio of dividends to the stock price, which indicates how much income you may receive from your stock. When looking at a particular stock, you can calculate its yield by dividing its annual dividend per share by the stock price. The result is reflected as a percentage, where a company paying a $5 annual dividend per share for a stock going at $100 will have a 5% yield.

A dividend yield should not be the sole metric by which any investor decides to put their money in. It should, most importantly, blend in with other metrics. If a company's yield is the only attractive metric, offering abnormally high yields, then the company might be in some trouble. Because you are a beginner, it might be crucial to steer clear of yields above 5%, or at least do your homework on why a yield is that high. This is because a high yield means more chunks of money taken out of the company's financials, potentially leaving it with less to survive in the long term. You always want your company to be in it for the long run.

Dividend Payout Ratio

This metric shows how much your company of choice pays dividends from its net income. After looking at a company's financial statements, you can calculate this metric by dividing the total amount of stocks by the company's net income.

If a company makes $200,000 in profits and its stocks amount to $50,000, then the dividend payout ratio is 25%. The trick to using this metric is to note that if the percentage is under 20%, too low, or 0%, then the stock is not a dividend. Similarly, anything above 50% is just as unsustainable as any ratio under 20%. Therefore, between 30%–50% is healthy.

Monthly Dividend Income

Because income and growth are critical components of short-term investments, this metric is critical for keeping you up to date on your returns. You can use platforms such as Sharesight to see complete reports on your future income based on your chosen dates and the dividends you uploaded there. Platforms like this break down your projected income into categories to see that you practice financial hygiene.

Cost Base of Dividend Reinvestment Plans (DRIPs or DRPs)

DRIPs reinvest dividends on your behalf in new shares to increase your exposure to a particular stock. You do not see any cash returns from your investments through such plans. The downside to growing your share size in any given company is keeping a record of it all. This is where you must consider using platforms, such as Sharesight, that help you keep a record of all your shares. On the bright side, you can increase your share size in a company without paying any further brokerage fees.

Total Annualized Return

This metric is essential to monitoring your portfolio's overall performance and health. It has fewer things to do as a dividend metric but holds just as much weight. When weighing an annualized return, you must take into account components such as time, brokerage costs, capital gains, dividends, distributions, and currency fluctuations. By taking this holistic view, you can better see which factors are affecting your return on investment and those that are negatively affecting it.

In addition to Sharesight, other available platforms will help you gather the necessary information to choose which dividends to go for. The platforms discussed below are popularly referred to as stock screeners. Through screeners, you can access information on a particular dividend by using filters such as revenue, profit margin, volatility, price/earnings (P/E) ratio, and debt-to-equity ratio.

You are also at liberty to search for stocks in your industry of choice. On most of these platforms, you will have to give information about your preferences. This way, the screen will reflect dividends that are catered for you. Screeners also eliminate the heavy paperwork and tedious tasks involved with keeping up to date with business- or economic-based news. Some screeners are free—offering you exactly what you will need to make an informed decision regarding dividend investments—while others require a subscription. Those you pay for often offer you more services that will greatly help materialize your wealth.

Top Screeners for Dividend Investing

Zacks

This platform makes its screens from estimated earnings revisions. This is because it believes that expert opinion on the performance of any stock will affect the stock in one way or another. As such, it focuses on the changes that financial analysts influence on a particular company's earnings to compile its estimates. The platform is popularly known for earning per share (EPS) estimates.

The platform has free access, kick-starting your journey with a free report. The current report that all newbies get is "5 Stocks Set to Double." Based on the information shared therein and the help it has been to your investments, you can then opt for a paid version of this platform. Premium subscribers, for instance, have access to screens that show momentum and growth. You can also create your own screen, filtering your portfolio down to your interests instead of having to read through a mounting number of indicators and stocks that are meaningless to you.

CNBC

This screener makes provision for Canadian stock exchanges and those in the United States. Their screens, therefore, have a wider reach. CNBC is among the best free stock screeners, often found in the shadows of dominant screeners such as Zacks. You can name, save, and even export your screen on this platform. You can narrow in on dividends in the health sector, consequently naming your screen after that. Then, you can filter out all dividends that are not in the industry. You can even narrow the current dividends of these companies to those with a 4% dividend yield.

After having narrowed it all down to what you want, you can save it either online or as a spreadsheet to keep revisiting and reconciling yourself with. You can even use categories such as growth trends and analyst estimates to filter your dividends on the screen. Because of its extensive filter categories, this platform is known as a microfilter.

Yahoo Finance

Yahoo Finance caters to you if you are not with a broker. Its screener shows a wide variety of information, ranging from live updates on the prices of gold, oil, and the like to stock-market-related news. The screener also focuses on growth stocks. Much like CNBC, you can create your own screen by filtering all your desired dividends into it. This platform allows for filters by sales to make it more beginner friendly. You can also put in the shared data as is to make a screen out of it.

FINVIZ

This platform is popular due to its relevance. This is because the platform's screener is known for portraying information on stocks that are currently the most popular (for the day). To give you this experience, it uses up-to-the-minute reports on major indexes such as the S&P 500 and Dow Jones.

Stocks are listed on this screener with their most recent percentage of change, value, as well as signal (which indicates whether they are strong gainers or losers; highly volatile; or even oversold). The stock screener is easy to follow, with stocks listed in alphabetical order with filters categorized as Fundamentals, Descriptive, and Technical. It is also beginner friendly, as it has a video that guides you to navigate your way around the platform and the investments thereon.

MarketWatch

If stock screens from the mentioned platforms overwhelm you with all sorts of data and specialized filters, you can count on MarketWatch to make stock monitoring a whole lot easier for you. This is because the platform's screener is highly organized and easy to find your way around. You can use the filter parameters that are easiest for you.

Most of the information portrayed on this screener can be narrowed down into technical, fundamental, volume, and even price. If you are looking into indexes, you will be sure to find the latest on this platform coupled with relevant market news.

It is important to look into a stockbroker once you have found the tool you will use to manage your investments. Brokers are responsible for ensuring your smooth trading of dividends. If you want to branch out and do your own research on the right stockbroker for you, make sure that it belongs to certain regulatory bodies. These include the Security Investor Protection Corporation (known as the SIPCS) and the Financial Industry Regulatory Authority. If the broker you choose also offers services like savings and checking accounts, make sure they are approved by the Federal Deposit Insurance Corporation (FDIC).

Investment Techniques and Strategies

If you opt for online trading platforms, there are two investment techniques at your disposal: a market order and a limit order. The type of order you choose will depend on your investment preferences.

Market Order

A market order is used by investors who want their orders to be carried out immediately. This is an essential kind of trade where a buyer buys a stock at or near the asking price set by the seller. On the same token, if you sell, you will receive the amount near or at the price you set up. It's important to remember that with a market order, the most important thing is how quickly the order is carried out; the price guarantee doesn't matter.

Orders here are carried out at current market value, meaning that the trade prices will vary. A trade price is a price paid to fulfill a trade order. Due to the fluctuating market, the trade price for one order is seldom the same as the last trade price before it. This can only be the case if the asking or bid price is the same as the previous one.

A significant advantage of using the market order to carry out a trade is that you can rest assured that such a trade will take place (the trade will be filled). Extra costs are usually associated with getting an order filled as quickly as possible.

Limit Order

On the other hand, a limit order is the direct opposite of a market order. A pending order, as some would call it, allows you to trade stock at a specific price in the future. However, the order will be filled when the price reaches the predetermined level. Unlike market orders, limit orders use the price as a critical feature to ensure that the order is filled. The limit part of things refers to the value you are willing to buy or sell. So, if you say you want to sell your dividend when it reaches $50 in the future, it will be sold once the price is achieved.

On the same token, if you want to buy a specific stock at $10, and then once the price for that stock hits $10, it is yours. It is an efficient way of trading, saving you from spending a cent more than you should. You can use this order to place orders on stocks that are not usually traded.

The four types of limit orders include the buy limit, sell limit, buy stop, and sell stop. The buy limit is used to place orders at or below the specified price. Placing the order at or below the market bid is essential for ensuring that the trade effects a price boost. A sell limit is used to place an order to sell at or above the current market ask. This way, the price is also improved. A buy stop is used to buy the stock at a price above the market bid. Working in direct contradiction with the buy limit, the buy stop depends on the stock reaching a predetermined price level (a stop level). Following that, the order will then be open to be either a market or a limit order. Lastly, a sell stop is used when a seller wants to sell stock at a lower price than the current asking price. Much like the buy stop, the order will become active once such a price has been reached.

The main downside to the limit order is that if the price never reaches your predetermined level, you lose out on ever buying the stock. There are other stock order types, all of which are aimed at ensuring that you play your cards right. These include the following:

Stop-Loss Order

Unlike market and limit orders, which remain active from the moment they are entered, a stop-loss order remains dormant and is only activated once the set price has been reached as a market order. This stock order saves you from manifesting a loss by immediately filing an order with the current market value. For instance, if you place a stop-loss sell order on stocks you hold in a particular company at $50 per share, it will remain inactive until the price reaches or drops below the threshold. This is when they are sold at the best available price. This is the best stop order to use if you do not have time to monitor the market. This way, you are saved from unfavorable downward slopes within the market. It may also be important to put a stop order on your stock before going away for a conference or holiday.

Stop-Limit Order

This stock order works the same way as the stop-loss order. However, the critical difference is that this order limits the price at which the order will be executed. Unlike the stop-loss order, which converts into a market order, the stop-limit order converts into a limit order once activated. As such, this order works on the stop price and the limit price. You must specify the price at which the stocks will be stopped and listed for sale. Then you must select the price at which the stores will sell. For instance, if you set a stop-limit order on shares you hold in a particular company at $50 per share and a limit order at $49 per share, then the stocks will be pulled out of your portfolio when they reach $50 and sold once the market price is $49. This may happen in a split second. Imagine that you initially bought these stocks for $30 per share; you have a $19 profit on each share sold.

The problem with this stock order is that you could lose out on gains should it be the case that the market recovers, and the shares you sold are now listed at higher prices. Overall, you should be careful when you use this stop order so that you don't end up with an unfilled limit order.

All or None

If you are interested in penny stocks, this stock order will come in handy in the future. Penny stocks are stocks from small companies that are listed on the exchanges. These stocks usually go for far less than the stocks of giant corporations. With an all-or-none order, investors usually seek to get the full quantity of the stock you requested. Through an all-or-none order, you are essentially placing an order for a fixed number of shares in a particular small company. If it just so happens that your targeted company is two shares short of your order, it remains unfulfilled, which is the downside of this stock order.

It is crucial to do extensive background checks on the company before executing an all-or-none order on its shares.

Immediate or Cancel

This stock order stipulates that a charge that can be filled within a matter of seconds be filled. Other parts of the order that cannot be filled immediately are then canceled. It prioritizes trades within an immediate interval. For instance, if you place an order for 500 shares, and the order cannot be filled in a matter of seconds, the order is canceled. It will help to use this stock order when processing smaller quantities of stock.

Fill or Kill

This is a combination of an all-or-none order and an immediate or canceled order. This order mandates that the entire quantity set out in all, or none be satisfied and that such an order be filled out immediately. If neither one of these aspects is satisfied, then the entire order is canceled. For instance, if you set fill or kill demand for 50 shares, it means that the 50 shares should be available from that company and that the order is processed within a matter of seconds.

Good 'Til Canceled

This stock orders caterers for a variety of stocks at once. You can set a time restriction for different stocks. When it has lapsed, you have the option to cancel them. Most brokerages allow for a maximum period of 90 days in which an investor can keep an order open. For instance, if you set a good 'til canceled order for 70 shares from a particular company and the order is not filled within the period set for it, it is canceled.

Day

If you do not set an expiry date for an open order through the good 'til canceled order, then the order will automatically be listed as a day order. This means that if the day ends without the order being filled, then it will expire. You can, however, re-enter the order the next day.

Take Profit

A take-profit stock order is used when you want to close an order at a profit. The order is fulfilled once the targeted profit has been reached. This is the most popular stock order across most investment opportunities, Forex trading included. It can be done as either an open position or a pending order that will be checked when the goal is met.

Chapter 5:

Online Trading Platforms

Online trading platforms exist for the sole purpose of your convenience as an investor. These platforms do away with the costly and time-consuming process of going to a broker's office to talk about investments. When paired with a screener that you can thoroughly understand, an online trading platform is a force for financial change. Online trading platforms offer lower costs when compared to top platforms for trading stocks with their hallmark minimum investment amounts coupled with zero flexibility. Because of this, online trading platforms are open to everyone—no matter where they come from or how much money they have.

Since there exists a heightened demand for stock trading, online trading platforms offer competitive prices—all to the benefit of the investor. Search perks include commission-free trading and little to no minimum trading amounts. Most importantly, these platforms cater to your needs as an investor and not to your own interests. One online broker can be known for providing a range of dividends to choose from, another for reliability, and the next for being beginner friendly. Below is a list of the best to get you started on your trading journey.

ID Ameritrade

This platform is the best online stock trading platform for beginners. Beginners can enjoy zero commission and minimum trading fees. However, transfer fees are due. This platform allows you the flexibility to trade by keeping the costs on your side. ID Ameritrade is also a research hub that is used to offer beginners some guidance. You can expect to see tutorials on how to go about your daily business on the platform and information about this platform on other media.

Due to its proliferation of research, ID Ameritrade provides you with a wealth of features to ensure that your trading journey runs smoothly. If you see yourself as a casual trader, this is your platform. Also, you'll have to pay a broker fee, which isn't too high compared to what you'd pay at a real stock trading platform.

E*Trade

On this platform, you can expect to trade without any minimums or commission fees. However, do expect to pay other transfer fees. This platform has a wonderful mobile application that is straightforward and, therefore, simple to navigate. The category for this platform is reliability. Because it is not aimed at beginners, it can be a bit of a hassle. This is mainly since it has been in the stock trading business for more than 40 years, but if you trust your learning skills, you might as well dive in and make the best of it.

Due to its longevity in the business, it has mastered the art of intelligent and relevant tools and services to keep it as reliable as it is. It has further provided users with exceptional information and educational support material to make your investment journey a breeze. It is also there for you to assist you in developing your own investment and trading skill set as well as make the most of your investment portfolio.

Merrill Edge

If you are looking for an online stock trading platform that will make your needs feel attended to in an extra special manner, then this is the platform for you. It is best known for personally supporting its users to unlock their investment genius and riches. It is integrated with the Bank of America, which explains why it offers personal support services that can only be found in elite financial institutions.

It also boasts an excellent research center, giving you access to the foundational concepts and investing principles to build yourself on. Their information center also caters to more advanced investors, often luring them in through intrigue. For a platform that pairs its services with one of the largest financial institutions, it surely does come at an affordable price. This is because you do not have to pay commission fees, nor do you have to pay minimum fees for your account. The transfer fees, however, do vary depending on your chosen options.

Fidelity Investment

This stock trading platform is a long-term investor's friend. It is best known for its future planning that is carried out at an affordable price. This is because you do not pay commissions and minimum account fees. However, you do pay some other account-related fees, which is standard for a platform in this niche. While its website is pretty dated compared to newer, more vibrant websites, it does win in the categories of beginner and family friendly.

Because its stock options are so diverse, it can pair investors with differing trading skills with the right stock options and portfolios for them. It is also big on research, which often births tools that make investing through it more efficient. This platform is so big that it is also recognized in metaverse-related investments such as the Roundhill Ball Metaverse ETF (METV). This platform will align your investment opportunities with your life objectives.

Interactive Brokers

If you are looking for a variety of investment options, then this is the platform for you. There are no minimum account fees on both the Pro and Lite version platforms. The commission fees, however, depend heavily on the kind of account you have with the platform and where you are located. This platform is for investors who want to push themselves and stay on top of their game. This is because it charges investors a fee for trading in low volumes. To avoid unnecessary expenditure, be sure to opt for this platform only if you are sure that you will be able to trade above the set threshold.

They have tools in place to help beginners better navigate the platform and its wide variety of investment opportunities. You can even purchase a fraction of a share on this platform, a feature only found in a select few of these platforms. Suppose all the administration involved in investing in dividends is a bit overwhelming for you. In that case, you can shed the load by investing in a portfolio compiled by specialized software. This portfolio is managed by way of algorithms alone, which is why it is referred to as Robo. It is a self-managed portfolio catering to your set needs and interests. This platform also offers Probability Labs to investors new to crushing investment-related numbers. You also have access to close to 50 courses to pick investment education from, which is one of the largest educational frameworks.

If you are not too confident navigating these platforms, you can create a demo account with any of those that offer and then trade in demo accounts. This way, you are not putting your money at risk of being lost. Alternatively, you can opt for a robo-advisor.

With a robo-advisor, you can expect to answer questions on your disposable income; how high or low your risk tolerance is; and your investment goals. Make sure to give detailed accounts, as this will result in more detailed help. Based on the answers you have given, the robo-advisor will create investment portfolios and suggest investment opportunities that are best suited for you. It can further manage these investment opportunities by rebalancing your portfolio to stay at the most lucrative point. It can further manage your affairs through measures such as tax harvesting, which lowers liability on your behalf.

With a robo-advisor, you can expect low stock trading fees, as the work is not done by a professional but, instead, by software. Most of the costs associated with using brokers with human labor are that the professionals must charge fees for the services. Another perk of having software as your advisor is the lack of conflict. This is because software serves your best interests, which might not always be the case with a human broker. This is because a broker might feel the pressure to promote sales of a certain stock due to the commitments it has to the company offering those stocks. The stock might not always be what is best for you.

The lowered minimum investment amounts go as low as $500, which makes for a more affordable commitment to trading. On top of that, the robo-advisor is always available since it is software and not a person. This means that anytime you need your advisor, they are there. There is no waiting for your call to be answered or being told that they are not available.

Chapter 6:

Top 10 Companies to Hold

Dividends Within

This is the part where you test the knowledge that you have acquired thus far. It isn't, however, mandatory for you to go dive into all the investments at once. You can, for instance, go one at a time, or you can afford to go. It might be the case that a few things have changed since the publication of this guide. Therefore, it is essential for you to go to your screener and find out if the company you have chosen from below is a good investment to make.

When doing your own research, you might find a few new companies listed among some of those listed below. You are at liberty to go for those companies since they too rank at the top. To trade these shares, place an order for the stocks' symbols directly on your trading platform of choice. The stock symbol is also referred to as the ticker code, which is a code comprising between one and five digits used to identify stocks. Find the companies listed below where you can begin honing your trading skills. Be sure to put their ticker codes on your platform.

CubeSmart (CUBE)

CubeSmart is a prominent self-storage company, the dividends of which would keep your wallet loaded. This is because self-storage is an asset class that can survive the gaps caused by market fluctuations due to its pricing flexibility. When there is a downward slope within the market, it is easy for the rent of the self-storage units to be increased. The monthly rental module used by this company creates a continuous influx of money, ensuring a steady flow of income. Also, the way companies like CubeSmart make money doesn't require a lot of physical labor, which makes inflation less of a problem in that area.

Another added benefit of investing within this company lies in the fact that it is a real estate investment. Real estate investment funds are also able to weather market storms such as inflation because of the heavy leveraging on their balance sheets when making property purchases. As such, as a CUBE stock owner, expect to see the value of the property you invested in increase in the face of absurdities such as inflation. Furthermore, you can expect to see the debt attached to your investment being inflated away.

Ambev SA (ABEV)

This Brazilian brewing subsidiary of the well-known "Anheuser Busch InBev SA" (brewing giant) is enjoying the current boom in commodities. Ambev SA is proud of its 3.7%, which is a reasonable percentage in the financial world. It dominates the South American market, some of which are also involved in the production of commodities that are recognized on a global scale. Brazil, for instance, is a force to be reckoned with in the production of commodities such as iron ore, oil, coffee, meat, and soybeans. Most of these commodities are enjoying a comforting degree of boom, which means that there is also a surge in the amount of disposable income within these regions. Therefore, more disposable income means more affordable beer itself. The strategic placement of this company will ensure a comfortable road for all investors in both the short and long run. With the World Cup taking place in November, it is only fair to predict a lengthy peak in returns on investments, since there was a surge in revenues as steep as 30% owing to the quarantine-related lift last year.

Suncor Energy Inc. (SU)

This is one of the leading companies in the energy and alternative energy, making it a good investment for anyone. The recent and sudden surge in oil prices put energy investors in favorable positions, with dividends that proved lucrative. Furthermore, the energy prices find unwavering support in the instability that has been unraveling in Eastern Europe. Besides the geopolitical mishaps, the market is also supported by giants in low-cost oil production. These are the main factors involved in keeping energy dividends as stable as can ever be.

Suncor is one of the biggest companies in the United States, specializing in integrated energy. Being the biggest of its kind in Canada, Suncor prides itself on its low-cost oil production that takes place in Alberta. It uses this oil as part of its integrated energy product. The oil sands in Alberta are the company's biggest assets, providing decades' worth of lifespan for Suncor and its investors. So, while Suncor gives the world reliable and stable energy, you can get dividends from the top league.

Gilead Sciences, Inc. (GILD)

This leader in the biotech industry welcomed this year with a shared tumble amounting to 15%. As bad as it looks, it is an opportune moment for investors to buy. This is because it is only a matter of time before the share prices pick up and the flight takes off again. It has been nearly 10 years since Gilead Sciences, Inc. furnished investors with a low price. This alone serves as an indicator of how strong the share price usually is. This drop has opened a door for investment in one of the biggest industries in the whole world: the pharmaceutical industry.

Knowing the size of the industry in which this biotech giant exists, the share price will soon surge and secure a satisfying dividend for every investor. If the price has been made up by the time you read this guide, know that investment in this company is still green. While many investors sold out due to one of the company's clinics' declines in sales due to a specific illness it was meant to solve (which was hepatitis C), the dividend yield is at a strong 4.8%.

VF Corporation (VFC)

This clothing and footwear company is known for footwear such as Vans, Timberland, and The North Face. The success of this company is reflected in the undefeated success that this company's footwear has shown within the fashion industry. This company is so successful that its sneakers are often a sign of financial stability within the community. The astounding success this company has achieved is also reflected in the fact that it has multiplied its dividends for 25 years. The company's shares have materialized by over 20% in a downward slope, which is why it is more affordable today than it was around seven months ago. Supply chain issues, combined with inflation (which caused the share price to fall), have created an opportunity for you to buy low and earn big dividends when the company catches up. After all, you can always count on dividends with a monetary value attached to them with a company such as this one.

Due to the growth in its dividends for the past two decades, VF Corporation is now known as a dividend aristocrat. This is what makes it an attractive investment for any investor. The mere fact that this company has withstood the test of time, especially in the ever-changing fashion world, is proof enough that any investor will reap satisfactory returns on investment for as long as this company continues to stand the test of time.

First American Financial Corporation (FAF)

First American Financial Corporation ranks as the second largest insurance company in the United States. It is standard for homeowners to get insurance in the form of a home loan (mortgage). Therefore, the fortunes of this company are closely tied to one timeless market. The housing market is one that will always exist for as long as human beings are alive. Therefore, with an investment in this market, you can look forward to receiving dividends for as long as there is human life. Through its dividends, this company will smoothly maneuver you into financial security through its second largest insurance company in America.

The sharp downward slope in the housing market is usually enough of a signal to send investors running and selling all housing-related shares. However, to turn their backs on this company during such dire times would be to make a financial mistake. Even in the face of rate hikes, this company still has the best interests of its investors at heart, with its stock selling at close to ten times its estimated earnings for the 2022 financial year.

Prudential Financial Inc. (PRU)

While the previously discussed company is in housing-related insurance, Prudential Financial dominates life insurance. While rate hikes elsewhere might send you packing, this is the exact place to be invested in should such a hike occur. After participating mainly in actions that involved trading sideways for years, this company has finally made waves of its own as a prominent life insurance provider. With its fortune set on hikes in interest rates, Prudential Finance has its eyes set on flying high along with its investors.

The share price is currently very welcoming due to the lack of accurate information surrounding the hike in interest rates. Insurance companies invest the policy premiums that their customers pay into financial assets of all shapes and sizes. When there is a change in interest rates, insurance companies get to earn a more satisfying spread on the investments they have made. Therefore, dividends in life insurance companies can even foresee an even more fruitful return on investment.

Citigroup Inc. (C)

Due to the dire effects that the pandemic had on people and markets alike, dividends in banks were not far-fetched ideas. Indeed, falling markets made it easier for investors to find and stick with their preferred financial institution. However, when lockdown restrictions were gradually lifted, the banks gradually made back the losses they had suffered from the pandemic. As a result, they ended up building up the strong share price that they once boasted about.

Therefore, it would be odd for a person to speak of investing in the giants of the banking sector post-pandemic. Furthermore, the hikes in pricing have been occurring for months now, which would make such a decision seem a tad odder. However, there are banks that have opted to try and keep things simple and normal for investors. For instance, Citigroup reduced its price from an astounding $80 to a reasonable $64 in the second month of 2022. As a result, it is still possible to buy into major banks within the sector.

Clorox Company (CLX)

When the pandemic broke out, there was a need for cleaning products—a need unlike any other before. This is where this company came in, saved the day, and made itself—and its investors—a fortune in the process. This phenomenon is what verified its position as a top-income stock, making it increasingly attractive as an investment opportunity. As society got a grip on the pandemic, the revenues that the company had grown accustomed to started to slope down. This company performed well prior to the pandemic but has yet to replicate that performance post-pandemic.

With factors such as inflation eating away at it, the Clorox Company has found itself in a position where it has to spend more on labor, raw materials, and logistics. Coupled with the decreased sales, this company is underperforming compared to its pre-pandemic performance. This provides the perfect window for a buy-in to the dividends it has to offer. Since it was a good pre-pandemic performer, it is only a matter of time before it goes back up there—this is especially true given that its name was prominent during a difficult period in society. Therefore, this is the perfect option for someone who wants to put their money in blue-chip stocks.

Unilever PLC (UL)

Like the Clorox Company, this global conglomerate is a trusted name within the consumer staples industry. Based in the United Kingdom, Unilever produces a vast variety of products found across a vast variety of categories. This company has a versatile production capacity that ranges from soaps to food, personal care, and even pet care. This versatility is what makes the dividends on these elite shares so high since they generate about $60 million annually from it.

There has since been a halt in its growth capacity, resulting in negative pressures on its profit margins. However, this trusted brand has attracted the attention of activists looking to spice things up and empower the company to break new ground. As such, you can trust that the share price is aiming for the sky. Therefore, this company is among the most coveted by investors.

These 10 companies provide any beginner with the necessary push they require to enter and comfortably navigate their way around, paying dividends in the future. Of course, the more an investor progresses, the more complex the data they will come across to reach an investment agreement or disagreement. These companies are all safe and will not only provide you with financial gains close to your heart but will also teach you how to observe the stock market.

However, if you decide to branch out and do the research and investment on your own, it is crucial to note that stock symbols also tell a story about the stance of the company. Usually, after the original ticker for a stock, an additional letter might be added. Below is a list of the letters to look out for when shopping for shares and what they mean. You might realize that you are not familiar with some of the terms below, and that is because they are not associated with the topic of dividends.

Letter	Meaning
A	Class A Shares
B	Class B Shares
C	The company does not meet the requirements to be listed on the platform but is temporarily listed

D	New issue of existing stocks
E	Missed SEC required filing(s) and can also be denoted using LF
F	Issued by a foreign company
G	First convertible bond
H	Second convertible bond
I	Third convertible bond
J	Voting share
K	Nonvoting share
L	Miscellaneous (lower class preference shares and warrants)
M	Fourth-class preference shares
N	Third-class preference shares
O	Second-class preference shares
P	First-class preference shares
Q	The company is in bankruptcy proceedings

R	Right offering
S	Shares are of beneficial interest
T	Issued with rights or warrants
U	Units
V	These shares are set to go through a corporate action plan that has been published
W	Warrants
X	Mutual Funds
Y	American depository receipt
Z	Miscellaneous
OP	Over-the-counter bulletin
PK	Pink sheets
SC	Nasdaq small cap
NM	Nasdaq national market

Conclusion

As can be seen, the first understanding that you, as an investor, must reach is that of your strengths and weaknesses. By focusing on one, or both, of these two factors, you are putting yourself into a more desirable situation. There is, therefore, no navigating the stock market as a computer. The fact that you are a human is reason enough to look in and see where and how you fit. The successful investor is always the observant one, after all. Having identified the kind of investor you are and strive to be, it is crucial to know the different investment opportunities at your disposal. If you skipped self-observation and learned more about the marketplace, it will probably show in your not-so-successful investment attempts.

Going into dividends as a beginner might be best navigated through a financial institution. This way, all the work that needs to be done is on their shoulders, and all you will have to do is invest money. While this is a stable way of achieving success, it is not the only way. It's also important to put some time and effort into learning things that will give you the tools you need to handle some of your investments on your own.

By the end of this guide, you must have come out as a mixed-term, or rather casual, investor. Based on your time and resources, you should have a plan to carry out your mixed-term investments. For someone who is tight on time, it is easier to leave long-term investments in the hands of trusted institutions while you find your way around short-term investments on your own. This way, you can achieve satisfactory returns on investments while also exploring dividends at your own pace. Eventually, you will be able to lift the weight off your income, making more space for leisure expenses (if you like).

If you are tight on resources like money, you can start with short-term investments. This way, you build your portfolio up to eventually be able to finance long-term investments. Short-term investments are also a time-consuming venture. Therefore, you should make it a point to schedule time to absorb all the information, make an informed decision, and monitor your choice.

As an investor, you must ensure that the decisions you make benefit you in the long run. This way, you have created a steady and reliable alternative stream of income for yourself. You have created a pathway to financial security and stability. However, it is essential to note that even giant corporations can crumble and fall in due time. Therefore, it is crucial for you to put your own hand into the mix—not just leave it to brokers to do it for you. When you've been through a loss, you'll know how to handle it better and how to avoid it in the future.

Given the various types of dividends available, it is critical to always aim for cash or stock dividends. These two dividends hold the monetary value that every investor wants to manifest. If you find yourself having to wait in line for your share of returns in a company that is liquidated, be sure to take notes on how it all went down. This is to see that you do not repeat the same mistake again. You want to stay clear of dividends like liquidating and property dividends, as these will weaken your portfolio and cost you more than they give.

Managing your portfolio by yourself is possible and is done by many individuals. You just must know what to stay clear of as well as the skills and techniques that you will mix into whichever investment strategy you are comfortable with. Also, it's important to stay away from people who offer to invest for you.

There are many misconceptions that you need to stay clear of. For instance, when looking at returns, it is essential to remember that high yields do not necessarily mean a good thing. Furthermore, a low price does not necessarily mean a good thing as well. In any form of investment, you must know why the share price is there. One share price could be negatively affected by the socio-political unrest around it, while another may be so due to the poor performance of the company. In the case of the former, it is easy to buy-in. This is because when there is trouble in a company's outside environment, the company has the chance to make corporate social investments to fix the trouble.

In the case of poor performance, there are varying degrees to consider before making your decision. If the company is in such a position because it failed to manage its finances properly, it is a sign for you to consider selling. Remember: You invested in the company for the sole purpose of gaining financial returns, and if a company starts showing cracks, then it is a danger to your finances as well.

It is a fact that not all decisions are made with the head. It might be that you chose to invest in the company because of shared values and sentiments. This might make it a bit of a challenge to abandon the ship should the company show cracks. Therefore, you have the option of keeping as many shares as you are comfortable with losing. This is to say that you should cash out as many dividends as possible and leave an amount that you are comfortable with losing. This way, you can monitor the performance of your company with the few dividends that you have left, and if the situation turns sour, then there is not much to lose.

An investor should avoid overextending themselves with every form of investment. This means that your finances should not be at the mercy of the market. No matter how tempting it is, keeping the threshold at 5% of your disposable income is lucrative. After all, it is not how much you invest that matters but how well you invest. Therefore, it is crucial to come up with a strategy for your investment. A strategy should always fit you, including your understanding as well as your means. Not formulating your own strategy puts you at risk.

Know when to use which stock order, know why to use it, and know when to use it. These are instruments for your success when navigated properly. Furthermore, use a screener to remain in the loop without having to sift through a lot of news that is not related to the market to find out what has been going on in the economy. Screeners also give out news on companies you focus on. Therefore, a good screener is your friend.

Technology has afforded you the perks of having brokers-only, software-generated ones included. If you want to learn more about dividends but don't want to hear a lot of different opinions, a robo-advisor is the best way to do that.

References

Adyta Birla Capital. (2021, September 17). *What are Shares and Types of Shares?* Adityabirlacapital.

    https://www.adityabirlacapital.com/abc-of-money/what-is-share-what-are-types-of-shares

Beers, B. (2021, April 22). *Market Order vs. Limit Order: What's the Difference?* Investopedia.

    https://www.investopedia.com/ask/answers/100314/whats-difference-between-market-order-and-limit-order.asp#:~:text=Key%20Takeaways-

Boyte-White, C. (2019). *How Dividends Affect Stock Prices.* Investopedia. https://www.investopedia.com/articles/investing/091015/how-dividends-affect-stock-prices.asp

Short-Term vs Long-Term Investors. (n.d.). Corporate Finance Institute. Retrieved April 4, 2022, from https://corporatefinanceinstitute.com/resources/knowledge/trading-investing/short-term-vs-long-term-investors/#:~:text=Short%2Dterm%20investors%20are%20investors

Divine, J. (2021). *15 of the Top Dividend Stocks to Buy for 2021*. U.S. News & World Report. https://money.usnews.com/investing/dividends/slideshows/best-dividend-stocks-to-buy-this-year?slide=2

Divine, J. (2022). *10 of the Best Dividend Stocks to Buy for 2019*. U.S. News & World Report. https://money.usnews.com/investing/dividends/slideshows/best-dividend-stocks-to-buy-this-year

Folger, J. (2020). *Do You Know the Right Way to Buy Stock? Market vs. Limit Orders*. Investopedia.

https://www.investopedia.com/investing/basics-trading-stock-know-your-orders/

Hayes, A. (2022). *Stock Symbol (Ticker)*. Investopedia. https://www.investopedia.com/terms/s/stocksymbol.asp

Leonard, T. (2020). *How free stock screeners can help narrow down your investing options*. TopTenReviews.

https://www.toptenreviews.com/best-free-stock-screeners

Leonard, T. (2021). *Best online stock trading brokers 2022*. TopTenReviews. https://www.toptenreviews.com/best-online-stock-trading-brokers

Mohan, P. (2021). *6 key metrics every dividend investor must track*. Sharesight. https://www.sharesight.com/blog/6-key-metrics-every-dividend-investor-must-track/

Understanding the Different Stock Exchanges. (2020). SoFi. https://www.sofi.com/learn/content/different-stock-exchanges/